START-UP ▲

FIDDLE

It's never been easier to start playing fiddle!

Published by
Wise Publications
14-15 Berners Street, London W1T 3LJ, UK.

Exclusive Distributors:
Music Sales Limited
Distribution Centre, Newmarket Road, Bury St Edmunds, Suffolk IP33 3YB, UK.
Music Sales Pty Limited
20 Resolution Drive, Caringbah, NSW 2229, Australia.

Order No. AM1003002
ISBN: 978-1-84938-990-7
This book © Copyright 2011 Wise Publications, a division of Music Sales Limited.

Adapted by David Harrison from an original book by Stacy Phillips.
Produced by shedwork.com
Design by Fresh Lemon.
Photography by Matthew Ward.
Model: Henrietta Haines.
Edited by Tom Farncombe.
Printed in the EU.

With thanks to Hobgoblin Music, London.

Your Guarantee of Quality

As publishers, we strive to produce every book to the highest commercial standards.
This book has been carefully designed to minimise awkward page turns and to make playing
from it a real pleasure. Particular care has been given to specifying acid-free, neutral-sized
paper made from pulps which have not been elemental chlorine bleached. This pulp is from
farmed sustainable forests and was produced with special regard for the environment.
Throughout, the printing and binding have been planned to ensure a sturdy, attractive
publication which should give years of enjoyment. If your copy fails to meet our high standards,
please inform us and we will gladly replace it.

www.musicsales.com

WISE PUBLICATIONS
part of The Music Sales Group
London / New York / Paris / Sydney / Copenhagen / Berlin / Madrid / Hong Kong / Tokyo

The instructions that follow are designed to get you started playing traditional fiddle music.

The difference between the fiddle and the violin is nothing more than the music they play. The instruments are identical, although some of the techniques have become specialised for classical or folk music.

Whether you want to play folk music from the British Isles, or old-time tunes from the Southern states of the USA, the fiddle is an exciting instrument to play, either on your own or in any combination of folk instrumentation.

The instrument's range means that you're always carrying the melody and puts you right out at the forefront of the music. In folk bands, fiddle tunes are often also played by mandolins, guitars, pipes and any other melody instrument, so you'll always have support before you go solo!

Once you've got your hands on a fiddle—and if you don't have one yet, be sure to get some help from a trusted friend in finding the right instrument for you—you'll want to start playing right away.

Each musical example in the book features a melody line that illustrates how fiddle technique is applied in a particular context.

If you're not familiar with music notation, take a look at the section on pages 38 and 39, where there's all the info you need to get up and running. Symbols that aren't defined in that section are explained as they appear.

Apart from the fiddle—and bow—there's hardly anything else you'll need. A decent shoulder rest is useful (especially if you're adopting a classical posture), and a duster for keeping excess rosin dust off the fiddle is a must. It won't hurt to carry some spare strings, and of course you should have some rosin: your music shop will be able to advise you and show you how to apply it.

So, tuck this book under your arm, hike to a secluded glade, abandoned tenement, or the comfort of your own home, and begin to fiddle away to your heart's content!

PARTS OF THE FIDDLE

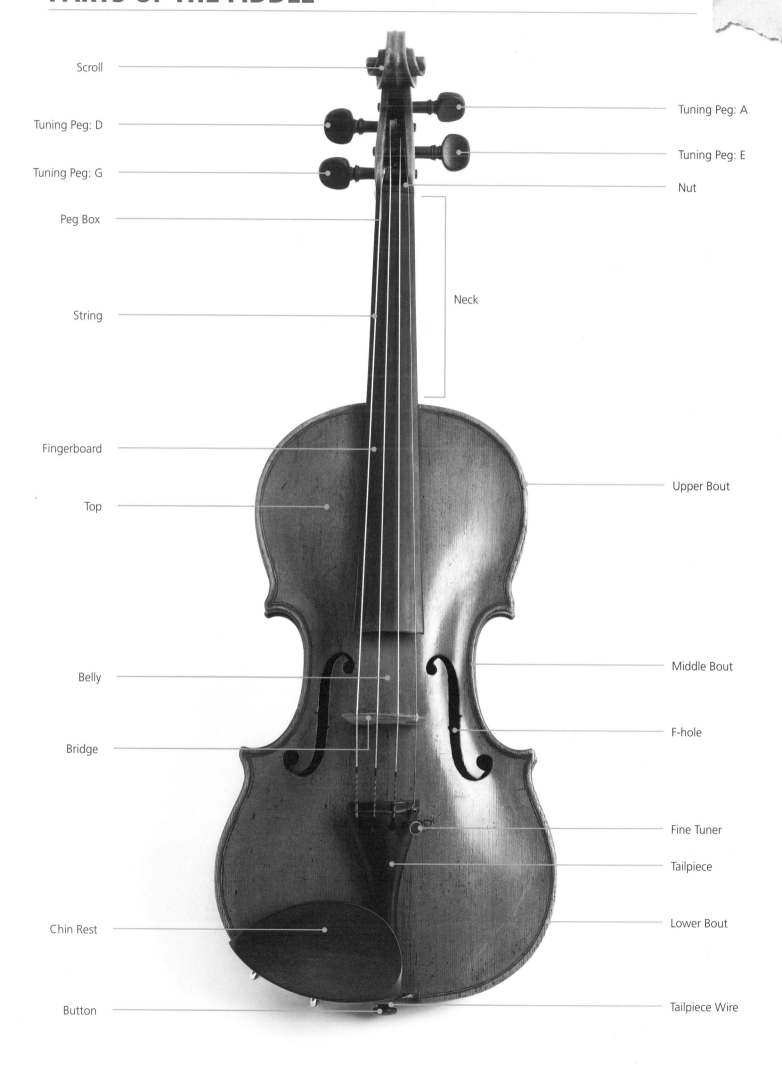

Scroll

Tuning Peg: D

Tuning Peg: G

Peg Box

String

Fingerboard

Top

Belly

Bridge

Chin Rest

Button

Tuning Peg: A

Tuning Peg: E

Nut

Neck

Upper Bout

Middle Bout

F-hole

Fine Tuner

Tailpiece

Lower Bout

Tailpiece Wire

HOLDING THE FIDDLE

There is no single, correct way to hold a fiddle and a bow, although the photos in this book should give you an idea of the various practical grips. If the method works for you, there is no need to conform to someone else's idea of how it 'ought' to be—just go with it.

Here are some general guidelines regarding grip:

● Keep both wrists limp. Tight fists keep the noting fingers from working efficiently, and prevent you from changing bow direction smoothly. If you decide to hold the violin against the shoulder (as opposed to your chest), hold it firmly between the left side of your lower jaw (not the point of your chin) and the inside of your left shoulder (not the top).

● Grip the instrument firmly between your shoulder and jaw. In this way, your noting hand is free to work the fingerboard. A shoulder rest will help hold the position.

If you play with the violin in the standard shoulder position, you'll need a shoulder rest (above).

● One advantage of holding the violin against your chest is that you can play and sing—or even call a square dance—at the same time.

You can hold the violin beneath your chin without any support from your noting hand, giving your hand freedom to move.

Here, the violin is held against the player's chest.

● Whether stading or sitting, ensure that you are
comfortable and remain relaxed. A good standing posture
requires even balance between the feet, an upright stance
and relaxed shoulders.

● If you'd prefer to sit, be sure to find a seat that offers
support without slumping. A stool like the one pictured is
ideal. Again, keep the shoulders and arms relaxed.

● No matter which method you use to support the fiddle,
don't let the neck rest in the hollow between your thumb
and forefinger.

Don't let the neck rest on the palm. Keep
it clear of your hand by supporting it
properly (opposite).

TUNING UP

The strings of the violin are tuned to E, A, D, G, respectively—beginning with the first, or highest, string and ending with the fourth, or the lowest, string. You can tune to another instrument, or use a pitch pipe, a tuning fork or an electronic tuner.

The strings are tuned to an interval of a fifth apart. That is, there are five scale steps between the E string and the A string—counting E as one, D as two, C as three, B as four, and A as five.

Similarly, five scale steps occur between the second and third strings—from A to D—as well as between the third and fourth strings—D to G. You will eventually learn to recognise the sound of this interval, and tune by ear.

At first, you may feel that it takes almost forever to get the strings in tune, but after a week or two, it should only take a couple of minutes.

Make an extra effort to tune out the last bit of dissonance before beginning to play.

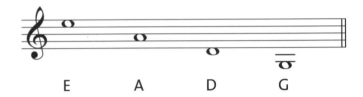

E   A   D   G

Many fiddles also have fine tuners installed on the tailpiece, which are especially useful for the thinner strings.

Tune the A string first, then the D below (listening to the interval between D and A). Now tune the bottom G string against D. Finally, tune the top E string by referring back to the A.

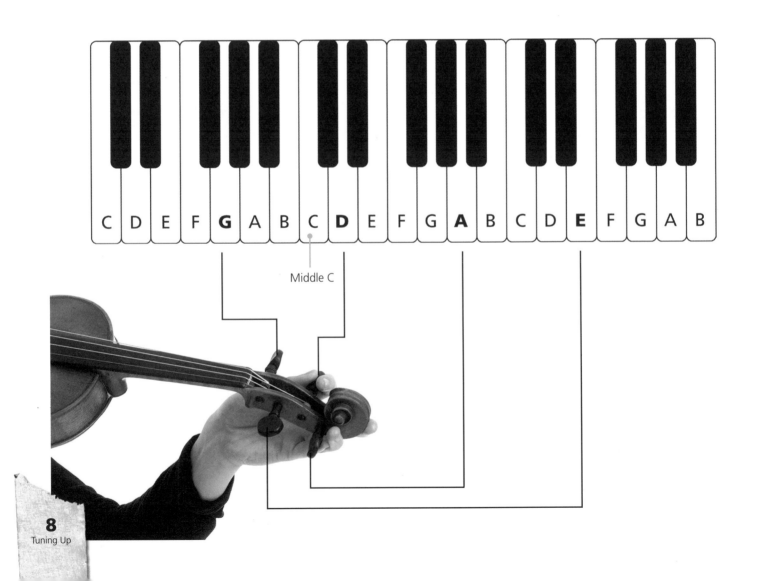

Middle C

THE BOW

Let's take a look at the violin bow and its components.

Lapping

Ferrule

Stick

Frog

Tip

Hair

Adjusting Screw

Some fiddlers hold the bow with the thumb in the space between the frog and the stick, with the fingers splayed on top of the stick (below left), while others place the thumb beneath the frog (below right).

Standard grip

Thumb-under-frog grip

The hair of your bow should be tightened so that it does not touch the stick when you are playing. Always relax the hair tension when you're not playing. The hair of the bow must be kept sticky with rosin, so that it catches on the strings. Without the rosin, the hair glides over the strings, and no tone is produced.

Rather than applying rosin before you play, put some on after you've finished. That way, the rosin will be 'set' for the next session.

THE BOW STROKE

Grab the bow and try playing some notes. You may either push the bow in an up-stroke (shown as $\vee$), or pull the bow in a down-stroke (shown as $\sqcap$).

Use the entire length of the stick as you play each tone in the example below. Make sure that you only make contact with one string at a time.

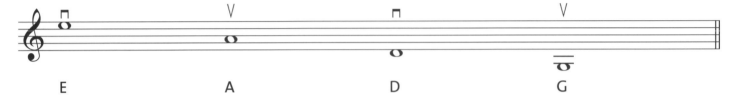

Now play the same example with reverse bowing—that is, substituting up-strokes for down-strokes, and vice versa.

The bow should be placed at an approximate midpoint between the bridge and the end of the fingerboard, and moved at a perpendicular angle to the strings. In fact, the bow should stay at a right angle to the strings for the entire length of the bow stroke.

The fiddle's tone changes according to bow placement. Some players like to place the bow a bit closer to the bridge, while others prefer it nearer to the fingerboard. Try to keep the bow from slipping up or down the strings during a bow stroke.

Let your elbow, wrist, and fingers do the work. Keep your shoulder relaxed, and don't jerk it around. Bow movement is mainly provided by the arm from the elbow down, so try to keep the elbow nice and loose.

Now let's compare the wrist position at the beginning and at the end of the stroke:

Keep the bow at right angles to the string throughout the stroke.

The wrist at the beginning of the bow stroke.

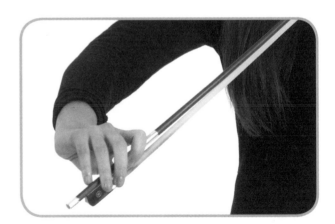

The wrist at the end of the bow stroke.

Your wrist should start to change direction just before the bow direction changes. The smooth execution of this wrist movement will help you to avoid making a choppy sound with each new stroke of the bow.

Of course, a smooth change is not always desirable, as you'll discover when we discuss *accenting* notes. For now, just focus on playing in a relaxed, smooth style as we move on to the left hand.

FINGER SPACING PATTERN ONE

The key of A is easiest to start with. The spacing of your fingers for an A scale on the B (second) and E (first) strings is shown below.

The dots on the diagram indicate where you should place the centre of each finger pad. The large spaces between the dots indicate whole steps, and the small spaces indicate half steps.

A combination of whole steps and half steps is needed to create a major scale. Now try the finger spacing for the A scale, as shown.

The numbers in the A scale (below) refer to the fingers that should be used to stop the indicated notes:

0 = open string; 1 = index finger; 2 = middle finger; 3 = index finger; 4 = little finger.

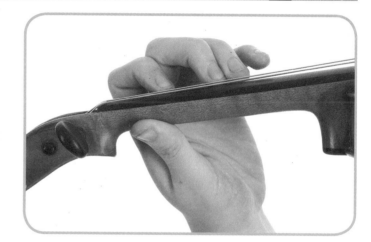

Finger spacing pattern one.

You will not need the little finger for this exercise, although it will be used later in the book. Start the scale with a down-stroke.

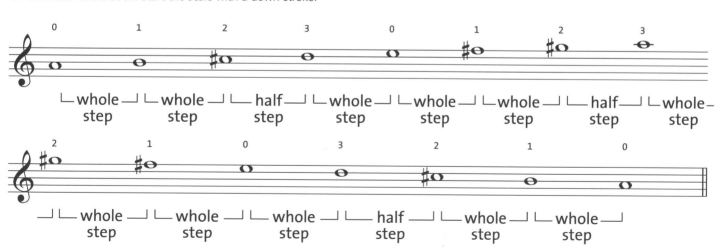

When you place the second finger down, keep the first down as well. When you play the D note, the first and second fingers should remain down. In order to minimise motion, try to keep any unused fingers hovering over the area in which they will soon be needed.

By the way, you should keep your fingernails short, to prevent them from gouging the wood of the fingerboard and to allow the fingertip to press the string right down onto the fingerboard.

THE KEY OF A

Practise the A scale until your fingers automatically fall into the correct spacings. Most accomplished players do not need to focus on their fingers. Through practice, they have developed an instinctive feel for fingerings and automatically avoid placing the fingers 'out of tune'.

The C, F, and G notes are always sharpened (raised by a half step) in an A scale. This information is notated the beginning of each staff in the *key signature*. Try playing this scale variation in the key of A.

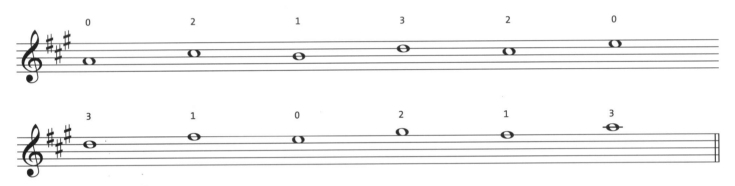

Now, try this descending variation.

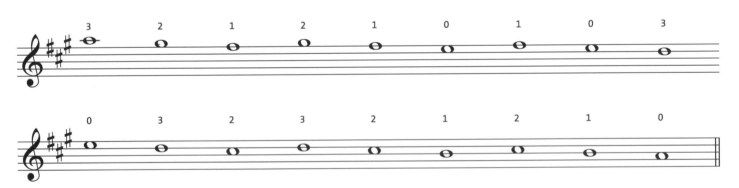

Facility with these permutations of basic scales is very important because many tunes incorporate these patterns.

It's time to try your hand at a complete tune in the key of A. 'On Top of Old Smokey' is a familiar favourite with a full one-octave range. Play one bow stroke per note, and make sure to hold each note for its full duration.

You can expect some squawks to occur as you play this tune the first few times. These are usually the result of too much bow pressure, or a stray finger touching a bowed string. If this happens, just pause for a moment and check that you are relaxed.

There are three beats in each measure.

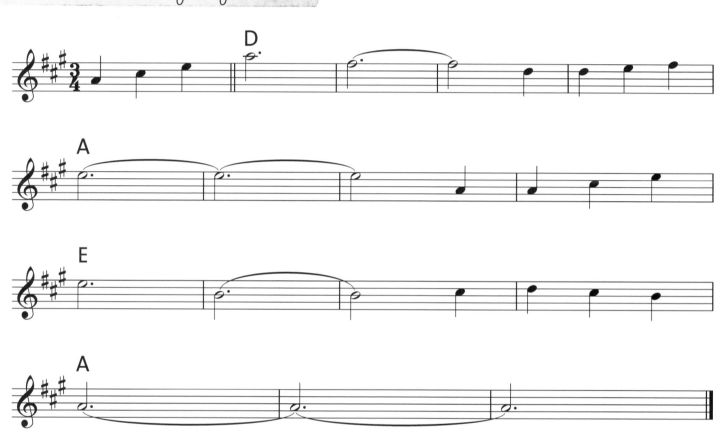

On Top of Old Smokey (Key of A)

Refer to the back of the book if you're not sure of the meaning of some of the symbols in the notation. The large letters are *chord symbols*, for guitar or piano accompaniment. The three notes before the double bar line are introductory notes that form a lead-in, or pick-up. The F♯ note that starts off the second measure is held for five beats: three beats are denoted by the dotted half note, and two more are indicated by the half note in the next measure. These two notes are attached with a curved line called a tie.

The E note that occurs two measures later is held for eight beats: that is, two dotted half notes (six beats), tied to one more half note (or two beats). Play these continuously with a single bow stroke. At first, you may have a tendency to move the bow faster than needed. As a result, you may run out of hair before eight beats are counted. Gaining the control to slow the speed of your bow stroke, and eventually increasing the tempo of this piece, will solve this common problem.

THE SINGLE SHUFFLE

When starting to play the fiddle, you may concentrate more on the correct placement of your fingers than good bowing technique.

However, bowing is central to good fiddling. To illustrate this fact, try playing the basic melody of the famous country song 'Boil the Cabbage Down'.

Boil the Cabbage Down

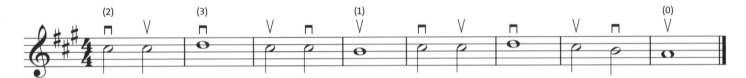

This somewhat drab melody may be made positively zesty with some bowing variations. The most common bowing pattern is a repeating cycle of long-short-short strokes. On the open A string, this cycle might occur as follows.

This pattern is called the *single shuffle*. Notice how the long bow automates between a down-stroke and up-stroke. The single shuffle pattern gives 'Boil the Cabbage Down' a traditional fiddle sound.

The key to getting a good single shuffle feel is to accent the first short stroke of each cycle. You can do this by increasing your finger pressure on the bow, or by suddenly moving it faster on the accented beat.

The prominence of this accent may vary according to taste and content—from a barely discernible volume increase to a sharp snap. Here is the single shuffle pattern, with marked accents:

As you increase the tempo, the accent pattern will sound more natural and propulsive. You will find that fiddle tunes with many short notes (like some of the breakdowns in this book), should be played using the middle third of the bow (or less). Some styles of old-time playing require only a couple of inches of bow per stroke.

This type of playing used to be referred to as *jiggy bow* fiddling. When playing in this traditional style, fiddlers like to *choke up* on the bow; that is, they hold the bow at a point high up the length of the stick.

As you move the bow more quickly, it naturally causes the strings to emit a distinctly different sound. During fast passages, you should use the middle of the bow. Your wrist should do almost all the work, while your forearm moves only a bit. For this reason, your wrist must remain relaxed and supple.

Choking up on the bow.

If, at this point, you're having trouble staying in tune, try any or all of the following:

● Occasionally check your tuning. Hard playing, temperature variations, and humidity can change the tension in strings. Make sure that your tuning pegs are holding firmly.

● Keep your fingers hovering just above the required finger spacing. Because your hand is probably not used to stretching, you may find that as you reach for one note, you will pull another finger sharp or flat. You may need to exercise your hand for a few minutes each day by gently stretching apart your fingers, so that their reach increases.

● If you grip the neck of your violin with your thumb, it can limit the stretching of your noting fingers. This is why both wrists must remain loose. Your chin and shoulder should support the instrument.

● Make sure that you press the strings down firmly.

The only things missing from a complete rendition of 'Boil the Cabbage Down' are a *kick-off* and a *tag*. The kick-off is designed to set the tempo for your fellow musicians, and give them a little time to get ready. The typical fiddle kick-off uses the form known colloquially as *potatoes* (perhaps, more accurately, *taters*). This traditional kick-off is usually eight beats in length (though it is sometimes extended to sixteen beats).

Remember the accent as you play the following single shuffle for kick-off to 'Boil the Cabbage Down'.

Any kick-off should be arranged so that the first note of the tune proper (that is, the first note after the double bar line) is bowed with a down-stroke.

Tags make other musicians aware of the imminent ending of the tune. They are not as formalised as kick-offs, but usually last eight beats. The familiar "shave-and-a-haircut-two-bits" song ending is a stock example of a tag. With 'Boil the Cabbage Down', the following tag may be added after the last measure of the final statement of the melody. This next example shows the last two measures of the tune, leading into an effective tag. Give this one a try:

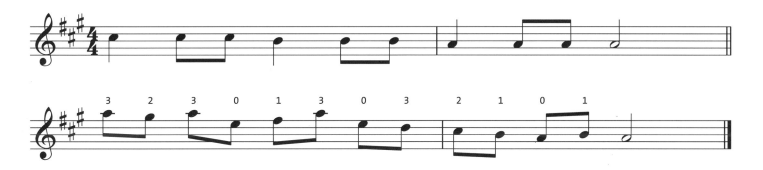

This tag may also be played with a shuffle rhythm, but here, two notes are played during the long bow stroke. A curved line that links notes of different pitches is known as a *slur*. This indicates that bow direction should not change for any of the connected notes. Try playing the tag again, with this in mind.

Now that you know the kick-off and tag for 'Boil the Cabbage Down', try playing the whole arrangement in tempo. Take the time to memorise this sequence.

THE KEY OF D

As you know, the interval between each adjacent fiddle string is the same. This means that you may use the finger spacing for the A scale (*Finger Spacing Pattern One*, page 11) to create a scale in the key of D.

To accomplish this, simply begin the scale pattern on the D string instead.

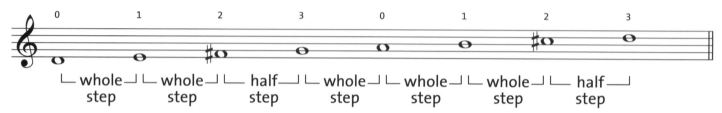

Once you're familiar with the scale, try playing 'On Top of Old Smokey' in the key of D. Notice that the new key signature only contains F♯ and C♯.

On Top of Old Smokey (Key of D)

FINGER SPACING PATTERN TWO

You should also be familiar with the upward extension of the D scale on the E string.

A different finger spacing is necessary to accomplish this: *Finger Spacing Pattern Two*.

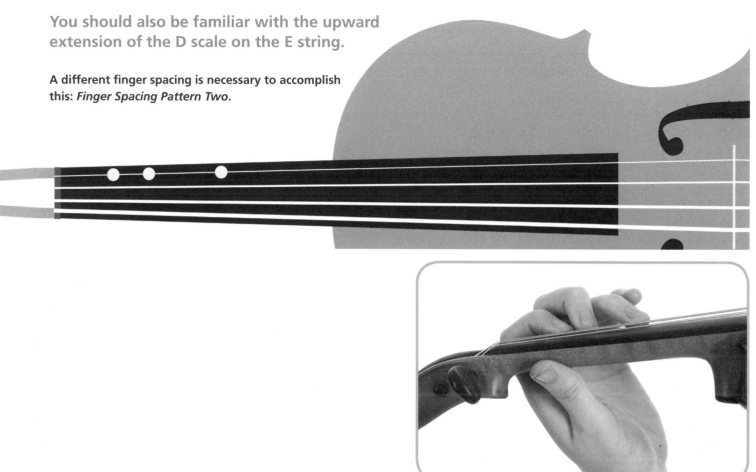

In musical notation, this extension would appear as follows:

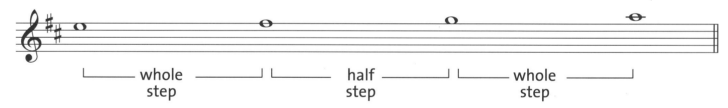

The arrangement of 'Mississippi Sawyer' on the following page has a typical fiddle-tune form—that is, two repeated sections.

The first section is played and then repeated before going on to the second section, which is also repeated once. You can use four 'potatoes' for the kick-off:

Try ending 'Mississippi Sawyer' with a tag similar to the one used in 'Boil the Cabbage Down':

'Mississippi Sawyer' introduces another basic fiddling technique called *rocking the bow*. As you can see from the first measure of the second section of the tune, this entails the use of alternating strings in a note series. Practise this technique using the open A and E strings.

Mississippi Sawyer

The rocking action of this technique becomes more evident when notes go by a bit faster. Try this technique in the next tune, 'Harvest Home Hornpipe', in which rocking is fundamental to the melody.

Harvest Hornpipe

'Harvest Hornpipe' is a Scottish/Irish tune that uses all saw strokes (that is, one note per bow). British tunes do not usually use kick-offs and tags, although these conventions do work well with many British tunes, too.

THE KEY OF G

To form a G scale, simply move the D scale down to the G and D strings, and apply *Finger Spacing Pattern One*. The low strings lend this scale a relatively dark, rich texture.

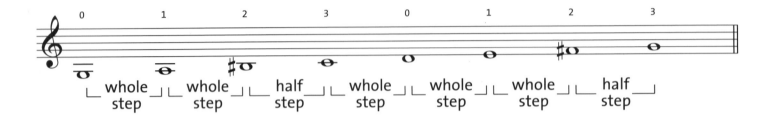

As with the D scale, *Finger Spacing Pattern Two* will here allow you to extend the G scale upward. Try extending this scale up another whole octave, plus one note. Note that the key signature of G contains only an F#. Start this extended scale with the last note of the G scale.

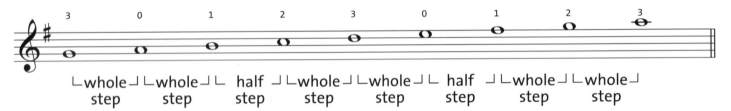

Here's a rather lengthy scale variation in the key of G. To make things more interesting, your little finger is now called to action.

The note played with the fourth finger should match the open string directly above. In fact, you may periodically compare the tone of the open string with the note played by the fourth finger to make sure that the stopped note is in tune.

Generally, the fourth finger is used instead of an open string for one of the following reasons:

- to slide up or down to a note;

- to make it possible to apply *vibrato* to a note;

- to avoid a potentially awkward bowing.

The single shuffle phrase (right) illustrates the use of the fourth finger where the open string would require an awkward bowing. Play this short phrase, as shown.

Clearly, it is easier to finger the A note than to switch strings (without changing the direction). The fourth finger must also be used in this way for scales that include no open strings.

'Muddy Roads' employs all four strings of the violin. The first section is in the key of G and the second section is in D. This changing key signature during the song is called a *modulation*. At this point in the song, C notes become sharpened (raised a half-step), so be aware of your finger spacings. Count four *potatoes* before you play this one.

Muddy Roads

SLIDES AND BLUES

Now let's add one of the fiddler's favourite ornaments—the slide (or *glissando*, as it is more formally known). This is an easy manoeuvre that can add lots of expression to your playing.

The blues is a typical setting for this effect. The basic blues is 12 bars (or measures) in length. In this style, the 3rd and 7th notes of the scale are often flattened (lowered one half-step).

Thus, in the key of G, the B and F♯ notes would become B♭ and F, respectively.

Start the slide with the fingertip somewhat flattened...

...and gradually raise the finger to its normal position as the pitch is reached.

In the G blues that follows, the diagonal arrows symbolise a quick slide (about a half step in length) up to the indicated note. Because the tone at the beginning of the slide is not held at all, it is not notated in the example. Start each slide immediately, and move quickly to the notated tone. Play these blues slowly, and bow it as you wish.

The G♯ note in the ninth measure of this tune is one half-step below the A note that follows. The last seven notes form a typical blues tag.

As you are dealing with quite a few accidentals in this piece, proper finger placement becomes important.

Blues in G

'Florida Blues' follows a typical blues form, but it is usually played up-tempo. When you encounter two consecutive slides (as in the first measure), you will need to move your fingers pretty quickly. Be sure to stop the bow between the two upward slides, so no downward glissando is discernible between them.

The B♯ note in measure nine is equivalent to a C note, and the E♯ in the 11th measure is the same as F.

The jagged symbol in measure 11 indicates a slide of definite length (via F♯ to E♯, or one half-step). Hold each note for the duration of an eighth-note. Try this tune.

As an experiment, turn back now to 'Harvest Home Hornpipe' and try to slide into the F♯ in the first measure. This will give you an idea of how this device sounds in a non-blues setting.

THE KEY OF C

The first note of the scale in the key of C is played with the third finger on the fourth string.

Finger Spacing Pattern Two is then employed as the scale continues up through the D and A strings. Here is the portion of the scale played on the D string.

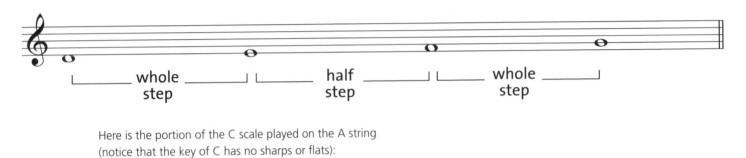

whole
step

half
step

whole
step

Here is the portion of the C scale played on the A string (notice that the key of C has no sharps or flats):

whole
step

half
step

whole
step

Let's play 'On Top of Old Smokey' again to get accustomed to this new scale.

On Top of Old Smokey (Key of C)

FINGER SPACING PATTERN THREE

When playing this scale below the C note, return to *Finger Spacing Pattern One*.

Extending the scale up to the E string requires a new spacing pattern.

Here's *Finger Spacing Pattern Three*.

Here is an extended variation of the C scale, with indicated finger spacing patterns.

The last few notes of this example require the biggest stretch yet your fingers.

Your first finger will probably need to be raised off the string when your fourth finger stops the B note. Try to keep the other fingers down. Some people with large hands can even extend the little finger up another half step to a high C.

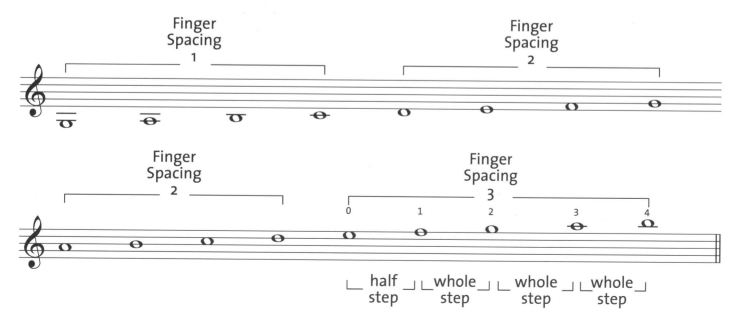

'Back Up and Push' begins with a slide for the fourth finger. The first three notes form the pick-up.

Back Up and Push #1

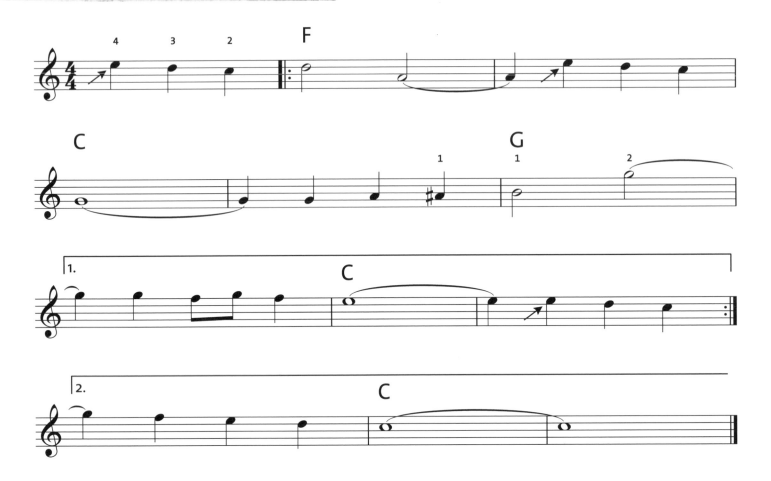

You will need to use some pretty long bow strokes to play the notes that are held for four beats or more. As you practise moving the bow at different speeds, you will notice that you are able to move it quite slowly and still produce a pleasing tone. As you play this tune, make sure to hold each note for its full duration. An A note occurs on the third beat of the first measure, and is held through the first beat of the second measure (a duration of three beats).

You may want to start this tune off with the standard 'potatoes' kick-off. If so, use one measure of 'taters' instead of two, as shown in the example below.

To provide contrast to the long bow strokes of 'Back Up and Push', fiddlers often add a shuffle section to the arrangement.

Try this shuffle variation slowly at first. Remember to change your finger placement when you play on the E string. You will find that this variation is a good exercise to develop your dexterity and playing speed.

The first two measures of this variation form an alternate second ending for the previous version. Here, a different three-beat pick-up is played to introduce the shuffle variation:

Back Up and Push #2

DOUBLE STOPS

Double stops are created when the bow rubs against two adjacent strings, and two notes are played simultaneously. Double stops provide a nice touch when added to the basic melody of 'Back Up and Push'.

The sounding of two identical notes is typical in traditional Southern fiddle music. When the two notes are truly in tune, they sound like one loud note. Here's a pick-up:

Try playing the open E string as the fourth finger slides up to an E note. The two strings, sounding together, add a biting accent to the beginning of the tune (this is also a good time to check that the little finger note is in tune). The sharp sound of the slide is dissonant (clashing) at first, then blends tunefully with the E note.

The '0' in the notation means that the E string is open. The '4' indicates that the A string is fingered with the little finger. Experiment with the speed of the slide.

If you get a squeaking noise when you try this double stop, you are probably allowing your little finger to graze the E string. Check your hand and finger positions, and give it another go.

'Boil the Cabbage Down' is a prime subject for some easy double stops. Run over the basic melody once again, and then try it with double stops, as shown:

This arrangement creates many opportunities for unwanted squeaks, so take it slowly and keep your wrists loose. Note the F♯ over the D note in the second measure.

Try each note of the piece in tune separately before trying the double stops. It will probably take a little practice before you are able to go from measure to measure without hesitation.

In the notation of the double-stop version of 'Muddy Roads' that follows, the open string drones are separated from the melody notes wherever possible. This unclutters the staff a bit and lets you follow the music more easily.

In this tune, the open string drones occur both above and below the melody. In the eighth measure, a D note on the A string forms a double stop with the open E. This is a somewhat dissonant effect, but is acceptable because it passes so quickly.

Muddy Roads (with Double Stops)

As you play the double stops, make the bow pressure equal on both strings to assure equal volume for the two notes that sound together.

Double stops are among the most challenging of fiddling techniques. As you experiment with them, you will find all sorts of note combinations are possible. Keep in mind that the tune may be in the higher or lower note of a double stop. Practise each note of the double stop and make sure they are both in tune before playing the two notes together.

Try playing the double stops shown below. Note that in each one there's a half-step spacing between the two fingers. Since they are on different strings, the difference in pitch is a sixth.

The first double stop in the exercise below is pictured here (right):

E and C double stop.

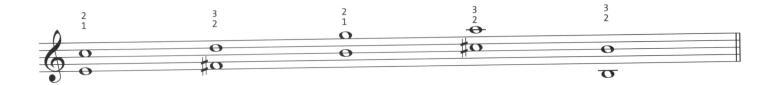

The three double stops that follow are similar to the one played in 'Boil the Cabbage Down'. They are pictured in turn below:

D and F# double stop.

G and B double stop.

C and E double stop.

Here are two sets of double stops, each of which works well as a 'potato' kick-off (right). Try beginning 'Muddy Roads' with either of these kick-offs.

 *etc.*

 *etc.*

Here are another couple of double stop kick-offs that will work well with 'Mississippi Sawyer':

 *etc.*

 *etc.*

Let's finish off with a few one-finger double stops. Here, the same finger must stop both strings. When you play these, you must keep the finger absolutely perpendicular to the string in order to keep both notes in tune. This variety of double stop may be tricky at first.

Take a look at 'Growling Old Man and Growling Old Woman' (page 35), which begins with a repeated one-finger double stop.

Now turn back to Blues in G and play it again with these double stops (right) added in measure seven:

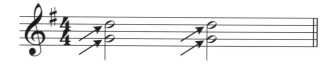

FINGER SPACING PATTERN FOUR

Extending the A scale down an octave onto the D and G strings requires a fourth pattern of finger spacing.

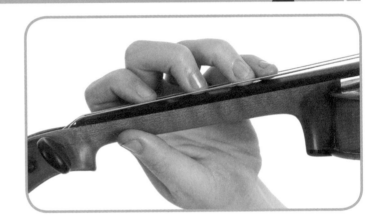

Beginning on the G string, the extended scale is as follows:

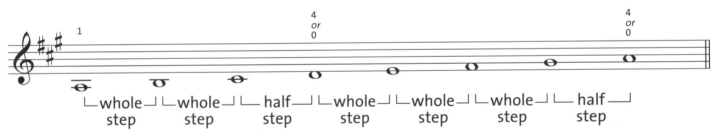

Combine this series with the A scale you have learned previously to form a two-octave scale:

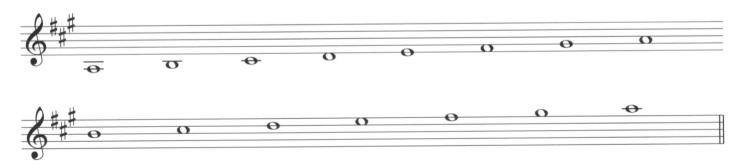

'Growling Old Man and Growling Old Woman' (opposite) is a challenging tune that alternates between a G scale and an A scale. You'll need to shift confidently between spacing patterns.

Remember that the key of G requires *Finger Spacing Pattern One* on the two lower strings, and *Finger Spacing Pattern Two* on the two higher strings.

This tune kicks off with a one-finger double stop. The tag features a rhythmic figure on the same double stop.

By the way, the lower part of this tune's melody is meant to represent the old man, and the high-pitched section brings to mind his female counterpart. Remember to emphasise the accents in this single shuffle pattern.

Growling Old Man and Growling Old Woman

Finger Spacing Pattern Four is also used on the A string when playing in the key of D, as in 'Arkansas Traveller'. Try this tune out for yourself.

Arkansas Traveller

READING MUSIC

Musical notes are written on a five-line grid called a *staff*. Notes can be written either on a line or in the space between two lines. The *pitch* of the note (how high or low it sounds) determines its position on the staff.

The fiddle can produce sounds lower—and higher—than can be written on the staff.

For these notes, *ledger* lines are used to provide a temporary extension to the staff: take a look at the first few notes in the example below to see ledger lines in action.

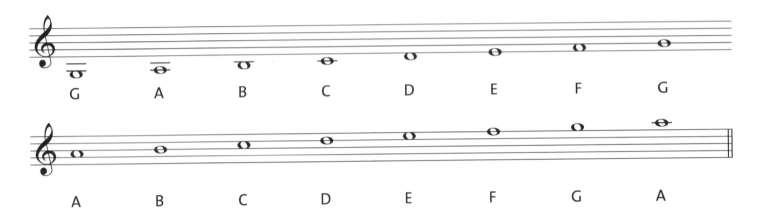

Notice also the curly symbol at the beginning of the staff, called a *treble clef* (right). The clef shows that the range of the music written is suitable for melody instruments, and all violin/fiddle music has a treble clef at the start of each line.

The staff is divided into groups of beats called *measures* or *bars* by vertical *barlines*. Reading the rhythm notation is pretty simple. Look at the beginning of a piece of music and you will see the time signature. The number on the top shows the number of beats per measure and the bottom number shows what type of note get one beat. A 4/4 time signature says that there are four beats per measure and a quarter note gets one beat. This is the most common metre in music.

There are five rhythmic values (kind of notes) that you need to know—whole notes, half notes, quarter notes, eighth notes and sixteenth notes. There are two eighth notes and four sixteenth notes to a quarter note, so in 4/4 an eighth note represents half a beat and a sixteenth note indicates a quarter of a beat. In the U.K. these rhythmic values are sometimes known by different names, and these are also shown in the diagram below. Notice the *double* barline at the end: these are used to divide sections of music up.

← beats per measure
← note that represents beat

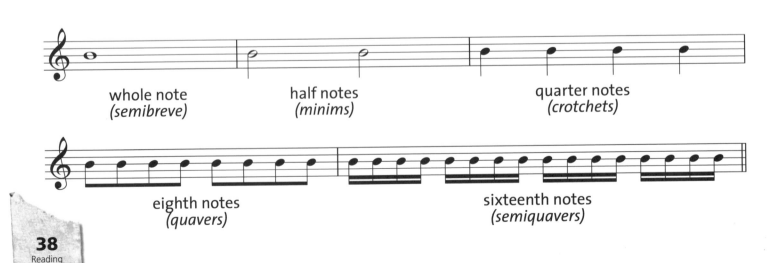

Note stems are drawn either up or down (right), depending whether the note head is above or below the middle line of the staff.

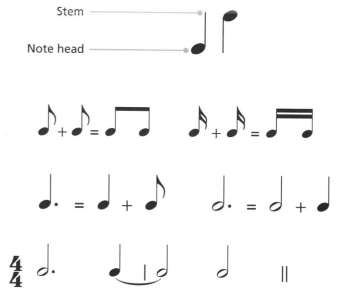

Stem

Note head

Eighth notes can appear singly, and where they are drawn in pairs they are joined by a beam (right). Sixteenths are joined by two beams.

A dot is used to lengthen the duration of a note by half. The dotted quarter note (right) is therefore worth one and a half quarter notes, or three eighths. The dotted minim is worth three quarter notes.

Notes that continue beyond a barline are notated as two separate notes joined by a curved line called a *tie* (right).

Where no note is played for a specific time value, a *rest* symbol is used:

whole note	half note	quarter note	eighth note	sixteenth note
(semibreve)	*(minim)*	*(crotchet)*	*(quaver)*	*(semiquaver)*

A sharp symbol (♯) raises a note by a half step. A flat symbol (♭) likewise lowers a note by a half step. When a note or notes are permanently sharpened or flattened throughout a piece of music, the symbols are shown as a *key signature* before the time signature at the start of the staff. In the example below, the key signature indicates that any F is played as F♯.

Where notes are temporarily altered up or down, sharp and flat symbols appear within the music. These are known as an *accidentals*.

Below, the third note is G and the fourth note is G♯, but this accidental is cancelled out by the natural sign (♮) for the next G.

Repeat bar lines (right) are placed at either end of a section if it's to be played more than once. In the example below, the repeated section ends differently each time. On the first time through, the 2nd bar is played, but on the repeat the music jumps straight to the 3rd bar—this is shown by the numbered horizontal brackets over the *first time bar* and *second time bar*.

Notice also the *final barline* at the very end of the piece.

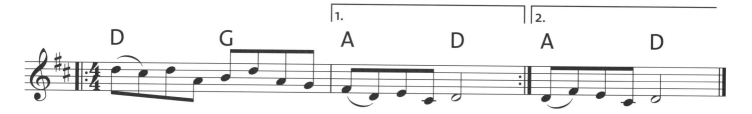

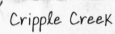

Cripple Creek

This Appalachian folk tune is often also played on the banjo and is a favourite of many bluegrass bands.

Home Brew Rag

This American tune features an F drone note on the top string in the first section. Keep the 1st finger in place where it appears.

Notice the new time signature: count two long beats in the bar.

Drowsy Maggie

Here's one of the best-known of all Irish reels. Notice the sixteenth-note triplets: groups of three played in the time of two.

Derry Hornpipe

Played a little slower than a reel, with a skipping eighth-note feel, the hornpipe originated in maritime folk music.

This time there are eighth-note triplets.

Hesleyside Reel

Here's an English reel from Northumbria, in the key of A. It should be played briskly with a steady beat.

McKenna's Favourite

Play the sixteenth note groups in this Irish jig in a single bow – in reality they're just fancy ornamentation.

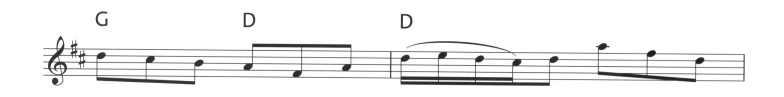

Frisky Jim

'Frisky Jim' is a hoedown, a virtuoso piece used in fiddling competitions. Take special care with the slurs.

Byrne's Hornpipe

Another Irish hornpipe: as before, play it with a lightly skipping rhythm. Count this one in four beats to the bar.

The Irish Washerwoman

Perhaps the most famous Irish jig of all, 'The Irish Washerwoman' is sometimes played repeatedly, with a gradually increasing tempo before a sudden stop.

· 1 2 3 4 5 6 7 8 9